The Courts Garden

Holt

THE NATIONAL TRUST

The Courts Garden, Holt

Looking through the Venetian gates to the cedar lawn and loggia

Allium *christophii* makes a great accent plant in any border. After flowering in May, the attractive seed head remains of interest long into the autumn

'The English Garden Style at its Best'

The Courts is a peaceful family garden with its roots in the past. From the bustling high street of Holt, you pass through an unassuming gateway into a quiet corner. A narrow avenue of pleached limes leads towards the mellow Bath-stone house – the 'hinge' around which the whole design of the L-shaped garden swings. From the house lawn, the garden spreads out in front of you.

In the tradition of Lawrence Johnston's famous garden at Hidcote, yew hedges and cones define the different spaces, but at The Courts it is all much more relaxed, so that one area flows naturally into the next. Vistas tempt the eye in every direction, but also create intrigue, as nothing lines up precisely. The stone edging to the borders hides subtle changes in level, and the stone pillars, the yew and box hedges, and the tall column on the main lawn give scale to the garden. The fertile soil, high water-table and mild climate all provide ideal growing conditions for the wide range of plants at The Courts. The choice was strongly influenced by the great garden designer Gertrude Jekyll in its luxuriance and subtle colour combinations, which are carefully maintained by the National Trust.

As the name suggests, The Courts was originally the village law court. The present house has been called 'an early Georgian gem'. It was built about 1720 for a wealthy cloth merchant from Bradford-on-Avon, who also manufactured cloth here. The water flowing through the garden powered his cloth mill, and the ponds in the eastern corner were used to dye the finished cloth.

The architect Sir George Hastings laid out the bones of the garden between 1900 and 1910. From 1921 two generations of the Goff family established The Courts' tradition of rich and varied planting, and in 1943 gave the house and garden to the National Trust. As no garden can stand still, the Trust has tried out new ideas in the same tradition.

Major Clarence Goff, who created the garden with his wife, Lady Cecilie, and gave it to the National Trust

The Smoke Bush (*Cotinus coggygria*) beside the Lily Pond

Early History: Cloth-making at The Courts

Holt is one of the many beautiful villages that lie along the Avon Valley to the east of Bath. In early times, it stood on the edge of Melksham and Selwood forests, which gave their name to the village, which means 'wooded hilltop'.

Around 1720 John Phelps, a Quaker cloth merchant from nearby Bradford-on-Avon, then one of the most prosperous wool towns in the valley, decided to build a house here, which is typical of the modest town houses of the area, but in this case set down in the country. (It is tenanted and not open to visitors.)

Cloth was also made here. The stream that flows through the garden provided the power and the water supply needed for the cloth mill, which stood just to the left of the house and was connected to it by a bridge. A larger pond was situated on the other side of the Bradford–Melksham road and a smaller pond near to the present entrance to the garden, linked by an underground stream. The water flowed into the cloth mill at the engine room, and the dye and water discharged into the smaller pond. The cloth made at the mill, by machine and hand-looms, was fine West of England broadcloth and was nearly always dark in colour.

John Davis ran the factory between about 1797 and his death in 1822, when the business was carried on by his widow, Sarah. However, the industry was in decline, and their son sold the factory in 1875. Both the mill and the house lay idle and empty for several years before 1888, when they were bought back cheaply by the Davises' grandson, William, who pulled down the mill and used the rubble to fill in two of the ponds. With the same stone he added to and altered the house, which was let out between 1890 and 1900.

The Courts in the 1880s, shortly before the cloth mill (with tall chimney in the centre) was demolished. This photograph was taken from the site of the shop in the village high street

William Davis with his family in 1879. In 1888 he bought back The Courts and pulled down the derelict mill

(*Opposite*) The entrance front of The Courts in 1943

The Making of a Garden

Sir George Hastings, who introduced many of the architectural features in the garden

Major Goff and his daughter Moyra standing in front of the Venetian gates, which they brought over from Ireland

(*Opposite*) The rear of the house in 1943. As a private garden, plants could be left to seed in the paving, which is not possible now. The planting comes right up to the house, and Agapanthus fills the pots

In 1900 Sir George Hastings, a well-known architect, bought the property and began making a garden. A designer rather than a plantsman, he put in yew, box and holly hedges, creating enclosures predominantly as a background for the stone ornaments which he brought from the Ranelagh Club in west London. To him are also due the architectural features, including the neo-Georgian conservatory, built in 1909 to his own design, and the classical temple situated beside the old dye pool.

In 1910 Sir George sold The Courts to the Misses Barclay and Trim. They were a striking pair – one short and tweedy, the other tall and elegant – who kept themselves to themselves and seem to have done little to the garden. The turning point came in 1922, when Major Clarence Goff purchased the property and moved here from Ireland with his wife Lady Cecilie and their children Moyra and Tom.

Major Goff was the grandson of one of William IV's many natural children by the actress Mrs Jordan. He had fought in the Boer and First World Wars and was to run the Holt Home Guard during the Second World War. In peacetime he served for many years on the London County Council. Lady Cecilie was the daughter of the Earl of Ancaster and had been brought up at Grimsthorpe Castle in Lincolnshire, where the park had been landscaped by 'Capability' Brown. She was a discerning gardener and plantswoman and over the next 30 years, with the help of her head gardener, Rupert Stacey, she established an intimate flower garden within the framework of immaculately clipped hedges laid out by Sir George. These hedges proved perfect for Lady Cecilie to practise

her philosophy that a garden should be a thing of mystery and not be seen entirely from one viewpoint. They also made ideal niches in which she could experiment with flower colour and texture. She believed a garden should be organised by colour, whether harmonising or contrasting.

Over many years of refinement, she perfected thrilling and dynamic associations. Some were generous self-contained set pieces; others played a supporting role, often employing colourful annuals to create movement and cohesion, which are so essential in planting.

Until her death in 1990, Moyra Goff was the Trust's tenant at The Courts. During the First World War she had worked for the Red Cross and in an aeroplane factory. Well into her eighties, she was still driving her AC Cobra sports car through the streets of Holt. She took a great interest in the garden, her main contribution being the planting in 1952 of the Arboretum, which shades the garden on its north and west sides.

In recent years, the National Trust has devised new planting schemes in the same spirit, including the Yellow and Blue Borders and the Hot Bed.

Moyra Goff at the wheel of her AC Cobra in the 1980s

Tour of the Garden

The Entrance

Although only 2.8 hectares (7 acres), the garden appears much larger, due mainly to the many hedges and also to the surrounding trees, which create a sense of depth. The garden has two main axes, south–east and south–west from the house. The first is more informal and contains the water garden; the second is much grander in scale and atmosphere.

As soon as you enter the garden, the scene is set. The first thing you see is a pleached lime avenue barely wide enough for two people, creating a visual tunnel terminating at the front door to the house. The paving stone came from Devizes gaol. Instantly you are beckoned forward, tempted to explore. At the end of the avenue the garden opens out invitingly.

Here, as throughout the garden, topiary is a recurring theme. Though planted symmetrically, each is clipped into its own idiosyncratic shape.

The Pillar Garden

Beyond a stone seat, restored by the National Trust in 1999, steps lead down to the Pillar Garden, so called because of the eight tall stone columns which until the Second World War had chains hung between, on which cloth was draped for drying. They are guarded by an ancient *Robinia pseudoacacia*.

Water is never far away. The rill, once an important element of the cloth mill, runs from here along the whole length of the lower garden into the Dye Pool. At various points you can cross by small bridges.

In the corner of the Pillar Garden under the shade of a majestic *Aesculus* × *carnea*, backed by bamboo (*Fargesia nitida*), and centred around a small pond is the fernery. Spring colour is achieved with *Helleborus orientalis*, *Galanthus* sp. 'S. Arnott' and 'Viridapicis' and *Erythronium tuolumnense*.

The Hot Bed

In contrast to the calmness of the Pillar Garden, the Hot Bed, which lies opposite, is planted with much stronger colours. Two *Taxus baccata* domes and four quince trees give structure to a planting of predominantly purple foliage with orange, red and yellow flowers.

Dahlia 'Bishop of Llandaff' in tandem with Verbena *bonariensis* is a terrific duo. The Verbena helps to support the more lax stems of the dahlia

Purple 'Queen of the Night' tulips are planted in the Hot Bed to produce an early spring display

Magnolia × *loebneri* 'Leonard Messel' thrives in the more shady parts of the garden. This is one to choose if your garden is on alkaline soil

The Courts house from the Pillar Garden

The Courts house
reflected in the Lily Pond

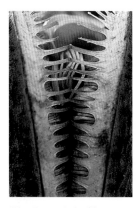

The dramatic looking
skeletal seedpod
Cardiocrinum giganteum
is a member of the
Lily family with flowers
reaching up to 2.4 metres
high

(*Right*) At each season the
temple vista is a delight,
none more so than in
autumn when the scene
smoulders in colours of
faded venetian

The Lily Pond

An enormous grouping of the Purple-
leafed Smoke Bush (*Cotinus coggygria*)
forms a dramatic background to the large
rectangular Lily Pond, which is surrounded
with *Iris sibirica* and Dierama *pulcherrimum*.
Throughout the garden, but especially
here, the leaf colours are quite brilliant in
autumn. Reds are provided by the *Cotinus*,
the *Prunus sargentii*, the *Acer griseum* and
Acer maximowiczianum. Yellows are seen in
the *Toona sinensis*, the *Koelreuteria
paniculata* and the *Heptacodium miconioides*.
The coloured fruits of *Crataegus persimilis*
'Prunifolia' and *Viburnum opulus* also
contribute autumn interest. Such an
impressive range of trees and shrubs
should inspire all visitors who share a
heavy limey soil.

The Dye Pool

From the Lily Pond, water flows into the
rill and from there into the Dye Pool at the
eastern corner of the garden. The
atmosphere here is shady, damp and
informal, almost jungle-like in flavour, with
an emphasis on foliage and texture. Several
large trees give an air of ancient peace.
These include Swamp Cypress (*Taxodium
distichum*), *Cercidiphyllum japonicum*, *Taxus*
'Dovastoniana', and, most spectacularly,
the two *Betula × youngii*, which are
reflected in the pool. Herbaceous planting
here features the shuttlecock fern,
Matteuccia struthiopteris, sailing like yachts
across a sea of blue *Corydalis flexuosa*.

The Temple Borders

Crossing a series of wooden bridges, you
arrive at the classical stone temple built by
Sir George. It rises from a bed of mainly
foliage plants such as *Rodgersia aesculifolia*,
Hosta sieboldii, *Aralia elata* and *Rudbeckia
maxima*. Situated at the end of a long
straight grass walk, the temple is flanked by
borders containing a backbone of gold-
leafed shrubs, roses (including *R*. 'Louise
Odier', *R*. 'William Lobb', and *R*. 'Fritz
Nobis') and herbaceous planting on a
yellow and purple theme, all backed by a
most curious holly hedge.

The Arboretum

At the opposite end of the grass walk to the
temple, two fine trees – a *Ginkgo biloba* and
a *Mespilus germanica* – guide you through a
gateway into the arboretum. Though only
planted in 1952, many of the trees are now
huge, thanks mainly to the very high water-
table. Of note are *Catalpa bignonioïdes* and
a stunning Cut-leafed Beech (*Fagus
sylvatica* var. *heterophylla* 'Aspleniifolia'),
together with young plantings of
Liquidambar styraciflua, *Liriodendron
tulipiferum* and others. In spring, many
narcissus cultivars emerge with *Fritillaria
meleagris* snaking between.

A bonfire of colour erupts throughout the garden but
especially in the arboretum in the autumn

The Terrace

From the Arboretum you can get back into the formal garden through the Venetian Gates. This splendid pair of wrought-iron gates of floral design was bought in Venice for £75 by Major Goff in 1912, and brought here from Ireland.

You can immediately sense that this area of the garden is much more formal than the lower water garden. However, the same recurring features are present, such as the 'Dancing Bear' topiary, the stone-work and the set-piece plantings. From here you can see the young plantings of *Cedrus deodara* (1988) and a *Morus nigra* (1999), both replacements of lost specimens. In time these trees will become the dominant feature, creating a seamless transition from the house, through the loggia to the garden.

Division of space is important in a garden of relatively flat terrain such as The Courts. Lady Cecilie relied upon hedges to do this. However, here she employed a different technique. A raised terrace was built, with the existing Conservatory providing a focal point at one end. She also erected eight metal columns at intervals, up which are trained alternatively the vines *Vitis coignetiae* and *Vitis vinifera* 'Purpurea'. A brilliant piece of design. To add even more height, the Trust has planted tall wands of ornamental grass, *Pennisetum macrourum* and *Stipa gigantea* on the terrace.

The Conservatory

Adjacent to the Conservatory, which is kept frost-free and houses an eclectic mixture of plants, is an area shaded by a large *Taxus baccata*. A spout drips water into a basin which flows into a small formal pond. Planting by the pond includes *Iris gatesii* 'Gerald Darby', *Coriaria japonica* and *Dryopteris erythrosora*, all of which revel in the cool environment. On the house wall nearby grow *Eriobotrya japonica*, *Shizophragma hydrangeoides*, fig and wisteria.

The Yew Walk

The most dramatic picture and appealing composition is yet to be encountered. This is the Yew Walk, which is punctuated on one side by yew cones, generous in size and repeated along the length to create impetus. The yews are echoed in the underplanting of mounds of *Santolina* that weave between them and contrast superbly with the much more fluid plant harmonies blended opposite. Keynote plants include *Crocosmia latifolia* 'Lucifer', *Achillea filipendulina* 'Cloth of Gold' and *Cephalaria gigantea*, all mingling with fill-in plants such as lilies and *Hemerocallis*.

Frost captured in the folds of a metal gate

Stone ornaments adorned the house lawn. The replacement cedar tree is beginning to imbue energy and height to this area

(*Left*) The 'dancing bear' topiary

(*Opposite*) The autumn garden is a thing of beauty, peopled by the towering seed heads of Digitalis and Eremurus with mounds of grasses at their feet

Onions in the kitchen garden

The Main Lawn

The immaculate expanse of the vast lawn is bordered on all sides with buxom plantings. The long border on the south side is planned for autumn interest with *Anemone* × *hybrida* 'Honorine Jobert' and *Fuchsia magellanica*. Further round, a deep semicircle of clipped yew provides yet another perfect niche for planting. Here the Trust has contrived a pink and blue harmony lightened with grey foliage and some white. Of particular note are the awesome flower spikes of *Eremurus robustus*, planted with the late herbaceous *Clematis heracleifolia*, which hides the leaves of the *Eremurus* as it dies down. To set off the whole scheme, a long bed is planted solely with *Festuca glauca*.

On the opposite side of the lawn cosseted in a south-facing bed is an effective combination of *Nandina domestica*, *Carpenteria californica* and *Euphorbia mellifera*, all underplanted with *Crinum* × *powellii* and contained within a fat box-hedged enclosure.

The Yellow and Blue Borders

The highlight of this area is the yellow and blue borders. Planned to have a seasonal blast in June, but still of interest at other times, with Salvias and Asters providing late colour. Two keynote plants anchoring the borders are *Miscanthus* sp. and *Crambe cordifolia*, both of which are left throughout the winter, together with others such as *Thalictrum*, *Agastache* and *Eryngium*, for feeding the birds and the aesthetic value of their skeletal forms.

The Sundial Lawn and Orchard

Up a flight of steps is the delightful Sundial Lawn – a perfect place to sit and absorb the spirit of the place. From here you can get into the Arboretum through narrow gaps in the yew hedge. You emerge firstly into an orchard, which makes a lasting impression of clever design simply executed. For here the Orchard acts as an ideal transitional space between the formal and informal parts of the garden.

Over recent years the gardeners have restored the large kitchen garden complete with herb borders, apple tunnel, pear espalier and nuttery. Recent plantings include a winter garden and bluebell walk.

Over 100 varieties of apple and pear are grown at the Courts.

Clipped topiary injects some order into the lush and exuberant planting schemes